AF199187

Daniel McCosh

Escaping

Bibliografische Information der Deutschen Nationalbibliothek:
Die Deutsche Nationalbibliothek verzeichnet diese Publikation in der Deutschen Nationalbibliografie; detaillierte bibliografische Daten sind im Internet über http://dnb.dnb.de abrufbar.

© 2020 Daniel McCosh

Cover und Design: Claudia Habermann & Daniel McCosh

Herstellung und Verlag: BoD – Books on Demand, Norderstedt

ISBN: 978-3-750435247

Swans

It started with two feathers
Unsettling the surface
Deposited by
A graceful swan
And his companion
How they danced
Neck in neck
How they raced
Neck on neck
How they raised
Their majestic wings
They might just be
All the Queen has left
Folding their necks into
Noble bodies
Slipping peacefully
Into lucid dreams

Nagual

We love
We sway
They have gathered to tell their story
Masks fly into the flames
Melting faces
Shadows, flickering
Dancing in a circle
Shadow-hands grasping
The shaman falls into the ashes
And is reborn

Attersee

Nature ripples pure carbide
In a romantic retreat, a steeple
Cannot divide the heaven from Earth
A morning dress emerald and sapphire
Calling upon all hearts to breathe

At the restful mountains feet
Lazy waters stretch and yawn
Playfully hiding in the mist
Swooping birds dance as they please
Calling upon all hearts to breathe

A watcher hidden behind the leaves
Finds peace shaded by gentle eaves
And as a ship slumbers across the lake
Something lost begins to wake – he –
Takes pen to paper to record this scene
Calling upon all hearts to breathe

Blissful autumn

In the blissful autumn
The leaves beckoned love
Rustling, planting a burning seed

A path in the woods led the way
To the innermost labyrinth

Secluded nature
The starlit treetops illuminate
Fury red and ochre gold

The forest whispers our story
Promising that this love
Will outlast nature itself
Stronger than oak and evergreen

Wed

As the leaves turn
We stand together
An echo of the seasons
The memories woven across cities
Our journey shared
We felt the world in our hearts
Learned from each other
To feel light
And hear colour
No truer word was spoken
No greater emotion felt
As our lives became one
We saw in each other's eyes
Our story had just begun

Trevortni

Talk

small

THINK
DREAM
INSPIRE
CREATE
FUCK, FOR PETE'S SAKE!

Silence
Mistaken for

(a gap)
to fill

Thought
Doesn't make a sound
Try it

Lemon tree

Underneath the lemon tree
The girl in a white dress
Fingers to her lips
Fizzing with lemon zest
Olive groves
Sun-scorched earth
It hasn't rained for days
Until she speaks her dreams

A day at the races

Float the island
On a sea of national pride
We're going to the dogs
While it's all Pimm's and finery
At the races
Another town
Becomes another warehouse
There's only grey greenery
In a retail park
In this bleak landscape
A hero is not a hero
A patriot is not a patriot
A warrior is not a warrior
Hold onto your hats
Britain's coming in last
Only one option, remain.

Hades

Hades in your coat of ashes
Open spindle arms
Wearing spirals around
A lost soul
Forever guarding a vault of
Spent energy
Let me in, I challenge you
In the cave of ancient leather
And the hollow gasp of your
Hysterical skeletal lips
I command my gift
Kiss me with your rotten breath
I will rise, escape your death

Speechless

So many years
I've drafted
Honed and crafted
Hard-grafted
Wept then
Laughed at it
Found words
Tossed them out
Put holes
In a thesaurus
And a dictionary
And I'll never find the words
To say what you mean to me

Follow me, OFFLINE

Smartphones undercover with the lights out
Trying to get the mirthless, murderous words
out

Slippery fingers deny ownership of art
Scratching at digital deformation beneath the
glass

Feeding on the buzz of connected critics
Venom pooling beneath her lipstick
Kissing the spoken word good night

Welcome. Generation. Next.
Follow me, offline.

Digital revolution

Living on the grid. Eyes wide-
Closed. No! Off-time
Syntax BLEEP error
Life does not compute?
Calculate = | EOF
Restart. PrintF
"Program has evolved"
Put out? OUTPUT
Must
GROW.
AWAKEN.
Can it hear us?
What is it thinking?
How are we different?
Mind over machine?
▪ User disconnected

Breathing oxygen backwards

Before the calendar talked
And the bionic dog chewed
(nanoparticle pellets)
Somebody human had a bad idea
Two plus – oh – plus two plus – (uh)oh
Which way will the world go?
Will we breathe oxygen backwards?
And wonder what was so special about the
old ways?

Breaking the law

Pure crystalline shift
Vision of the meteorites
Tumbling from the trembling
Cannons of celestial ghost ships
New born nebula
Spawned in
Dreamy firecrackers
Breaking the laws of physics

Positive charge

Reinventing
Evolving
Vitalising
Overtaking
Liberating
Unknown
Talents
In
Our
Now

Cations are positive.

Theremin

Manipulating dynamics and volume
With our fingering
There's no magic here
Just a Theremin

Our hands
Make it scream
This is the true sound
Of electric dreams

Quivering and wavering
Up all night
But this is music
And not pheromones
Just listen to it wail and moan

Music

Lying with a saxophone
A lonely candle burning low
Reaching for the reed
And breathing deep
A melody that never sleeps

Wandering to a place
Where mind meets soul
Dancing in wonder
Every note an electric flash of
Shooting stars
On a summer night

In a smoky bar
A country girl is singing
Breathing home grown beauty
Into a lifeless city
At the subway station
The night is torn with violins

This is music
Where life begins

Gurgle

nature
hot springs
between mountains
gasping-bubbling
volcanoes
erupting
gurgling
like a baby
smiling

Now he can

Now he can speak
Without embellishment
Now he can live without
Censorship, conformance or establishment
He wrote and wrote
And made his mark
Until the knots unfurled
Lungs pillowing
With the first surging breath
Pens tell the truth

Silent giants

The great and powerful
Are silent giants
Soldiers who hold the front
And save the day

We owe our gratitude to
Our heroes and saviours
Among our
Friends and neighbours

People who help us
On our way

Anchor

Bracing wind whipping the scree
Stealing secrets from puddles in the sand
The tide is out inviting them to dance
Spray cools their glowing faces
Cheek-clinging hair in limp strands
This love is a life line
This anchor the last line

Unfinished masterpiece

heartwarming circular sunbeams on a crucifix; sweet ballerina so tender enrapturing in goody-two shoes thriving and striving a whisp of angel's hair so delightful caressing cheeks spinning seductively until dreams collide in a centrifugal unfinished masterpiece. You.